D0745630

CAVING

CAVING

ODYSSEYS

JIM WHITING

CREATIVE EDUCATION

Published by Creative Education
P.O. Box 227, Mankato, Minnesota 56002
Creative Education is an imprint of The Creative Company
www.thecreativecompany.us

Design by Blue Design (www.bluedes.com)
Production by Joe Kahnke
Art direction by Rita Marshall
Printed in China

Photographs by Alamy (AF archive, Clint Farlinger, Moviestore
collection Ltd, Gavin Newman, Anna Omelchenko, Photos
12, Rowan Romeyn, Robbie Shone), Creative Commons
Wikimedia (Nicholas Frost), Flickr (BevoStevo), FrontierFolk.
net (Jon Hagee), Getty Images (Axelle/Bauer-Griffin, New
York Daily News Archive), iStockphoto (Ramil Iusupov,
Jens_Lambert_Photography, salajean), National Geographic
Creative (SISSE BRIMBERG, DAVID S. BOYER AND ARLAN
R. WIKER), Shutterstock (Marco Barone, catalin eremia, FCG,
salajean)

Library of Congress Cataloging-in-Publication Data
Names: Whiting, Jim, author.
Title: Caving / Jim Whiting.
Series: Odysseys in outdoor adventures.
Includes bibliographical references, webography, and index.
Summary: An in-depth survey of the history of caving, as well
as tips and advice on where to find caves, how to prepare, and
the skills and supplies necessary for different types of caving.
Identifiers: LCCN 2016031801 / ISBN 978-1-60818-690-7
(hardcover) / ISBN 978-1-56660-726-1 (eBook)

Subjects: LCSH: 1. Caving—Juvenile literature. 2. Caving—
History—Juvenile literature.
Classification: LCC GV200.62.W55 2017 / DDC 796.52/5—dc23

CCSS: RI.7.1, 2, 3, 4, 5; RI.8.1, 2, 3, 4, 5; RI.9-10.1, 2, 3, 4; RI.11-12.1,
2, 3, 4; RH.6-8.1, 2, 4, 5; RH.9-10.2, 4, 5

First Edition 9 8 7 6 5 4 3 2 1

CONTENTS

Introduction

Adventure awaits! It's a call from Mother Nature heard by nature lovers and thrill seekers alike. This temptation beckons them, prompting them to pack their gear, pull on their jackets, and head out the door. From mountain peaks to ocean depths and everywhere in between, the earth is a giant playground for those who love to explore and challenge themselves. Not content to follow the beaten

OPPOSITE: With proper safety equipment and lighting, a group of cavers can confidently explore the mysteries of an underground cavern.

path, they push the limits by venturing farther, faster, deeper, and higher. Going to such lengths, they discover satisfaction, excitement, and fun. Theirs is a world of thrilling outdoor adventures.

For some, this adventure takes the form of descending into the earth to explore caves. It can be frightening to enter total darkness and crawl through tight spaces with only a flashlight to guide you. There are several terms to describe people who enjoy this activity. Perhaps the most common is "spelunker," derived from a Latin word meaning "cave." However, many people who are serious refer to themselves as "cavers." They regard spelunkers as people who are often unprepared for risks and may even need to be rescued. No matter what they call themselves, though, there's no question that cave explorers are doing something extreme.

The First Cavers

For countless thousands of years, humans sought shelter from the elements, from predators, and even from each other by living in caves. These rocky openings often made the difference between life and death. Caves offered a number of advantages as ready-made shelters that featured relatively consistent temperatures year round.

Eventually, of course, humans stopped living in caves. But even

then, they stayed close to the cave entrances. Beyond the feeble light from fires and candles, the depths of caves were regarded as places of magic, mystery, and horrifying monsters. After a group of ancient Greeks went into a cave in search of silver, the Roman philosopher Seneca wrote, "They saw huge rushing rivers and vast still lakes, spectacles fit to make them shake with horror.... They live in fear, for tempting the fires of Hell." This attitude persisted at least through the late 1600s. Entering a cave in England in 1694, clergyman James Brome noted, "We then thought certainly we were arrived upon the Confines of the Infernal Regions ... Although we entered in frolicksome and merry, yet we might return out of it Sad and Pensive, and never more been seen to Laugh whilst we lived in the world."

Gradually, such fears subsided. People started

exploring caves, fascinated by the wonders revealed to them. The first one to become well known was Austria's Adelsberg Cave. People flocked to it after Austrian Emperor Francis I visited there in 1818. To accommodate the increasing number of curiosity seekers who began plumbing its depths, workers installed graded paths, stone steps, and lanterns. Within half a century, 8,000 people visited every year and stayed at nearby hotels.

A Kentucky hunter following a wounded bear in 1790 discovered Mammoth Cave. This was the first major cave to be explored in the United States. At first, its chief value was as a source of saltpeter, an important ingredient in gunpowder. But by the end of the 1800s, it had become increasingly popular as a tourist destination. So popular, in fact, that it spawned the so-called "Cave Wars" early in the 20th century. Owners of competing smaller caves in Kentucky tried to draw off some of Mammoth's would-be visitors. As regional historian Dave Tabler notes, "Mammoth's rivals went to dastardly lengths to lure tourists to their underground cash cows. They placed misleading signs along the roads leading from Cave City to the Mammoth Cave. They diverted tourists with fake policemen, employed stooges to heckle each other's guided tours, burned down ticket huts, and put out ... advertisements ... that Mammoth Cave was closed, quarantined, caved in, or otherwise inaccessible."

Eventually, the conflict died down. By that time, technological advances such as nylon ropes, improved lighting, and lightweight aluminum ladders began to make caving safer and attracted more enthusiasts. Founded in 1941, the National Speleological Society (NSS) sought to put caving on a more scientific basis. Calling themselves speleologists, NSS members studied the geology and biology of caves. In particular, they dispelled the idea that caves were barren, lifeless places. It soon became evident that caves are teeming with life, if you know where to look. Mammoth Cave, for example, is home to more than 130 different animals, birds, amphibians, and fish.

The NSS also discovered how caves are formed. The majority of caves are in areas composed of lime-stone rock. They begin as solid rock. Over thousands of years, carbon dioxide from the earth's atmosphere and from dead plants and animals mixes with water in the ground. This makes the water acidic. As the acidic water seeps into naturally occurring cracks, it breaks down the limestone. Eventually, the cracks get larger and form underground holes. As the holes expand, water begins flowing through them. The water carries sand and tiny rock particles, which wear away even more limestone and create underground passages that can become several miles long.

As water continues to drip from the top of a cave, each drop leaves behind a speck of the mineral calcite. These specks accumulate to form stalactites, tubular-shaped rocks that descend from the ceiling. Sometimes drops that still contain calcite fall to the cave floor. As the water evaporates and years go by, the accumulated

Mammoth Cave

Mammoth Cave is the world's largest cave system. It was occupied by humans more than 6,000 years ago. After its "discovery" in the late 1700s, it was privately owned for nearly 150 years until becoming a national park in 1941. Today, it is a World Heritage site. Because its temperature remains between the high 50s and low 60s, tours are offered throughout the year. As part of the tour, rangers like to turn off the lights. After a few moments of total darkness, they light a match to show how even a tiny bit of light spreads through the blackness. No one knows just how large Mammoth Cave is. While 10 miles (16.1 km) are available for tours, more than 400 additional miles (644 km) have been explored, and cavers are constantly discovering new passages.

calcite inches upward to form stalagmites. There's an easy way to remember the difference between these two formations. Think of the "g" in stalagmites. These grow upward from the *ground*. Similarly, the "c" in stalactites can stand for *ceiling*, where they originate. Many times, stalagmites and stalactites will meet and form a single structure known as a column.

There are several other notable types of caves. Lava tubes are formed during volcanic eruptions. As lava cascades down a volcano, the outer part of the flow hardens rel-

atively quickly. The lava on the interior continues its downward path and leaves behind a cave as it finishes draining.

The constant battering of ocean waves can create cracks in seaside cliffs. As the waves continue breaking into the rock, the pressure of the water and the sand it carries slowly enlarge the opening. Then a cave slowly develops.

When large stones fall from the walls of a valley, they may collect in a stream bed at the bottom. The stream hollows out a gap beneath the boulders, which becomes larger over the course of many years. At the same time, further erosion of the slopes adds dirt and more stones on top of this boulder cave. The growth of trees, grass, and other vegetation creates a certain amount of stability. However, there is always the danger that some of the boulders may shift and tumble into the stream bed. Exploring this type of cave is definitely not for beginners!

Ice caves form in glaciers or other areas with ice hundreds or thousands of feet thick. During warm weather, meltwater forms streams and rivers that flow into deep, open cracks called crevasses. This hollows out caves. Ice caving requires extreme care and the use of special equipment such as crampons, or sharp metal spikes attached to boots for traction.

Caves are commonly made from limestone or shale rock. Other caves are formed from flowing lava. Still others, such as that pictured, are carved in the ice of a glacier.

Gearing Up and Going Down

If you're just starting out in caving, it's best to wear old clothes over a layer that will keep you warm. A **synthetic** fabric that will wick moisture away is a good choice for this inner layer. So is lightweight wool, since it will retain heat even if it becomes wet. You can also try lightweight coveralls, since you're likely to encounter water. Some of it drips from the ceiling, and these drips are likely to form pools along the

OPPOSITE: A caver uses safety equipment, including ropes and a helmet with a light mounted on it, for a successful and more secure trip into a cave.

cave floor. You may even need to find your way through some underground streams. Don't wear cotton, because it absorbs sweat and water and will quickly become clammy.

Running shoes or sneakers may be all right for show caves—caves that are open to the public—which often (but not always) provide guides to take you through the passages. But for serious caving, you'll need a good pair of hiking boots. Those not only provide protection against twisting an ankle on an uneven surface but also superior traction, especially if the surface is wet and

slippery. Wear woolen socks. They provide warmth, even when wet. You'll be miserable if you wear cotton socks and they get wet.

Gloves not only help keep your hands warm but can also aid in gripping, especially in tight quarters where you need to pull yourself along. A leather palm on the gloves can help. Rubber gloves are good if you anticipate significant amounts of water. Cotton is a poor choice, not just because it will remain saturated as soon as it gets wet, but also it wears out quickly, even in dry caves.

Since you're likely to do some crawling, be sure to take knee pads and elbow pads. Start with normal athletic pads for these two key areas and then move on to customized caving pads.

Then there's safety equipment. Do not *ever* venture into a cave without it. Nothing is more important than

Most experts recommend taking at least three light sources—one as your primary source and two backups.

a helmet because falling rocks are one of the primary potential sources of injury. You can purchase or rent a helmet specifically designed for caving. A bike helmet is also a good choice.

You need light. Plenty of light. Most experts recommend taking at least three light sources—one as your primary source and two backups. Some caving lights are designed to fit onto a helmet to keep your hands free. You can also carry a flashlight. Be sure to pack replacement batteries for both types of devices. You should also carry a candle or two and waterproof matches. Wearing a watch with a luminous dial helps keep track of time. One useful tip is to use a watch that beeps at regular intervals, such as every half hour or every hour. It's easy to be so caught up in the experience of caving that you lose all track of time. The regular beeps provide useful reminders of how long you've been down.

Don't neglect nourishment or hydration. Bring as much water as you can comfortably carry. Caving can be surprisingly strenuous and create thirst. High-energy snacks are also a good idea to keep your energy levels up.

n addition to the proper equipment, experienced cavers emphasize several safety rules you absolutely need to follow to make your experience as risk-

Danger in the Depths

Cave diving is perhaps the riskiest form of caving. The 927-foot-deep (283 m) Boesmansgat (Bushman's Hole) in South Africa illustrates the dangers. During a practice dive there in 1994, 20-year-old Deon Dreyer disappeared. Ten years later, David Shaw discovered Dreyer's body while setting a world depth record. He couldn't free the body from the silt it had fallen into. Shaw felt obligated to return. After a year of planning and recruiting support divers, Shaw went back to Boesmansgat. A head-mounted camera recorded what unfolded. He became entangled with the body bag he brought with him and his light went out. The effort to free himself in the utter blackness caused him to overexert. He passed out and died. Still intertwined, the two bodies floated to the surface.

free as possible. The most important thing is to never go into a cave by yourself. In fact, don't ever go with fewer than three people in your group. In the event of an injury, one person can remain with the victim while the third immediately seeks help. Even though you have companionship, make sure that an adult who is not part of your group knows where you are going and when you expect to return.

While in a cave, don't run or jump. Many caves have slick and/or uneven surfaces, and you could suffer a serious fall. Also refrain from drinking cave water without purifying it. You have no idea what may be in it, and you may get very sick. Avoid going caving when it's raining because caves are subject to flooding.

Once you're suitably equipped and have taken the precautions outlined above, you're ready to start. Just keep one thing in mind: think of caving as a case of the hare and the tortoise. Always picture yourself as the tortoise. Even something seemingly as simple as walking winds up being more complicated because of the darkness and the likelihood of uneven surfaces. As mentioned above, taking it slow and steady is best. For example, if you're stumbling, you're probably moving too fast. If you do have to use the sides of a cave to keep your balance, try to a) put your hands only where others have already touched, and b) if possible, use your fingertips rather than your entire hand. Most of the time, you will want to go headfirst so that you can see what lies ahead. But if you come to a pit, go down feet-first.

As the best chess players do, always try to think a few moves ahead. And always think about conserving energy. For example, if you snag your clothing on something, stop

and slowly back away to try to free it. Bulldozing ahead can rip the clothing and thereby increase the possibility of further snags.

Almost certainly you will find yourself crawling at some point, especially when you get to narrow passages. In very tight places, you can get through more easily if you exhale. If you are wearing a backpack, remove it and push it ahead of you through the passage. Don't try to go through first and then drag it behind you. The amount of twisting you would need to accomplish that can gobble up lots of energy, and the pack could get snagged.

If being in tight spaces is frightening to you, keep that in mind while caving. It's not unreasonable to begin with those feelings. Such fears often reduce with experience or even go away altogether. Like all other aspects of caving, be patient and don't try to exceed your comfort level.

A Cautionary Tale

Édouard-Alfred Martel was just
seven when his parents took him
to the Caves of Gargas in the
Pyrenees Mountains between
France and Spain. That ignited
a lifelong love for caves. After
becoming a lawyer as an adult, he
left that profession and launched
his formal cave-exploring career in
1888 at the age of 29. Seven years
later, he founded the Speleological
Society, the world's first scientific

caving organization. During his lifetime, he documented more than 1,500 cave explorations. He is known as the "Father of Modern Speleology" for his groundbreaking efforts. He summed up his philosophy as follows: "No man has gone before us in these depths, no one knows where we go nor what we see, nothing so strangely beautiful was ever presented to us, and spontaneously we ask each other the same question: are we not dreaming?"

"Dreaming" turned into a nightmare for Floyd Collins, almost certainly the world's best-known caver. In 1917, Collins became involved in Kentucky's "Cave Wars" when he discovered Crystal Cave. After a year of hard work to develop the cave, he and his family opened it to tourists. Unfortunately, it was so remote that hardly anyone visited it. Collins spent several years trying to find connections with more accessible caves.

In early January 1925, he thought he'd achieved his goal when he discovered a narrow opening leading downward to what later became known as Sand Cave. He was working his way through his discovery several weeks later when his lantern went out. Pushing off in the darkness with his feet, he dislodged a rock from the ceiling. It pinned his left ankle and foot inside a tiny chamber about eight feet (2.4 m) long and no more than a foot (30.5 cm) high. As he struggled to free himself with his right foot, dirt and stones cascaded down on him. Both of his legs and feet were pinned.

The next day, Collins's anxious family discovered his plight but couldn't free him. A local newspaper sent 21-year-old reporter William Burke Miller to cover the story. Miller decided to get firsthand information. His small size—5-foot-5 and 117 pounds—made it possible for him to squeeze through the cave's narrow passageways. "I had to squirm like a snake," he wrote. "Water covers almost every inch of the ground, and after the first few feet I was wet through and through. Every moment it got colder."

iller's story—and several subsequent ones as he visited Collins every day, bringing food and water—created a sensation. An estimated 1,200 newspapers carried Miller's accounts, topped by blaring headlines. The new medium of radio also got into the

While Floyd Collins was trapped in Sand Cave, radio announcers interrupted regularly broadcast radio programs to deliver hourly updates for the nation.

act, issuing bulletins several times a day. As a result, Collins became one of the era's most significant media figures. The frenzy attracted massive crowds to the site. "The public's fascination with the story reached its peak when approximately 50,000 people came to Sand Cave 9 days after Floyd had become trapped," says Michael Crisp, who made a documentary film about Collins in 2014. "Nicknamed 'Carnival Sunday,' the large crowd featured families who had arrived with a **morbid** curiosity about Floyd's fate, as well as food and beverage vendors, preachers, and other onlookers." Churches throughout the nation held prayer vigils for Collins.

Hundreds of would-be rescuers tried desperately to free Collins. At one point, he reportedly asked for his foot to be amputated. It would have been nearly impossible to tackle such major surgery in such a confined space, anyway. The local fire department thought it could fit a harness and pull him out. Miller managed to attach the harness, but when the rope tightened, Collins screamed, "Stop! I can't stand it! It's pulling me in two!"

Perhaps the best opportunity came when Miller used an automobile jack, crowbar, and wooden blocks to try to dislodge the rock. The device initially eased the pressure, but the blocks kept slipping out. Tired, chilled to the bone, and discouraged, Miller finally returned to the surface. He was fortunate. Soon afterward, a cave-in blocked all access to Collins. He was alone in the darkness, cold, and increasingly hungry and thirsty. The next step was to dig a vertical shaft nearby, and then cut across to where he was trapped. After several days of frantic, round-the-clock efforts, the rescuers reached him. He was dead.

When Floyd Collins entered Sand Cave, he went alone. He carried only one light source and wore no helmet. He did not even tell anyone where he was going. If he had taken proper precautions, his story might have had a different ending.

The Missing Leg Mystery

Floyd Collins's saga didn't end when his body was removed from the cave and buried. His family sold Crystal Cave in 1927. The new owner had the body dug up and placed in a glass-topped coffin at the cave entrance. Guides gave lectures about Collins while tourists gawked at his remains. His family objected, but a judge sided with the new owner. Two years later, the body disappeared. Searchers found it in the bushes nearby, wrapped in a burlap bag. But his left leg was gone. After that, the coffin was chained and locked every night. No one ever found the missing leg. Crystal Cave closed in 1961, with the coffin still inside. In 1989, Collins's remains were reburied in a cemetery.

With the risk of cave-ins still very real, it took two months to retrieve Collins's body. The men also pulled out the rock that had trapped him. Some exaggerated reports maintained that it weighed up to 7 tons (6.4 t). In reality, it was just 27 pounds (12.2 kg)—a weight Collins could have easily managed under any other circumstances. Today, the inscription on his tombstone reads, "Greatest Cave Explorer Ever Known." It might be more fitting to use part of the **eulogy** delivered by a minister soon after his death that also linked him in spirit

WILLIAM FLOYD
COLLINS
BORN
JULY 20,1887
BURIED
APRIL 26,1925.

TRAPPED IN SAND CAVE,
JAN. 30, 1925.
DISCOVERED CRYSTAL CAVE,
JAN. 18, 1917.
GREATEST CAVE EXPLORER
EVER KNOWN.

with Édouard-Alfred Martel: "He was a lover of caves who saw in the gigantic formations and in the fantastic patterns on the way the traceries of God."

The publicity surrounding Collins's death was a double-edged sword. On one hand, people throughout the country became much more aware of the Kentucky caverns. On the other, potential visitors feared that even such well-established caverns as Mammoth were unsafe. In the long term, though, cave systems in Kentucky and elsewhere became increasingly attractive to tourists.

Because caves are so immense and seem so solid, it can be hard to realize that, in many ways, they are quite fragile. And damage can be irreversible. Cut down a tree, and another may soon grow to replace it. But that's not true with caves. Their "growth" often takes thousands of years.

Cut down a tree, and another may soon grow to replace it. But that's not true with caves. Their "growth" often takes thousands of years.

Caves today face several threats. One is pollution. Polluted water seeps into the limestone, containing chemicals that can break down the formations and destroy living things that inhabit the caves. Many of these cave dwellers are already on the edge of extinction. People may also dump their trash by cave entrances, which introduces foreign elements into the caves.

Caves can also fall victim to too much love. As more people swarm into caves, they can destroy in a careless moment what may have taken centuries or even longer to build up. All visitors should follow the motto of the NSS: "Take nothing but pictures, kill nothing but time, leave nothing but footprints."

The most famous part of New Mexico's Carlsbad Caverns is the Big Room. The ceiling is 255 feet (77.7 m) high. At 2,000 feet (610 m) long, it's large enough to easily hold 6 football fields.

Caving in Contemporary Culture

Caves and caving have always exerted a powerful grip on our imaginations. This is reflected in many aspects of pop culture, such as books and movies. In *Trixie Belden and the Mystery at Bob-White Cave* (1963) by Kathryn Kenny, Trixie and her family visit her uncle, who lives in a cabin in the Ozark Mountains of Arkansas.

Trixie is looking forward to exploring a series of caves. A national magazine is offering a reward to anyone who can find a ghost cave fish. Trixie wants to win and won't let anything stand in her way—not even the ghost that people tell her haunts the caves.

An 11-year-old named Tom Hammond rushes out of his home one evening at the start of Nathan Wilson's book *Leepike Ridge* (2007). He rides a large foam raft down a river and disappears into an underground cave, where he has a number of adventures. He wants to return home, but treasure hunters are chasing him. Many critics compare this Tom with the character of Tom Sawyer in Mark Twain's 1876 novel *The Adventures of Tom Sawyer*.

Author Penny Warner's Girl Scout Troop 13 series includes *Mystery of the Haunted Caves* (2001). Four Troop 13 friends with **complementary** skills—Becca (computers), Sierra (nature), C. J. (puzzles), and Jonnie (sports)—want to win the Gold Rush Jamboree. A mysterious clue sends them into a nearby cave system in search of buried treasure. But they're not alone. Hundreds of bats fly around them. And a group of robbers have their eyes on the treasure, too. They don't want the girls getting in their way. The book won several Best Juvenile Mystery awards.

Gertrude Chandler Warner's Boxcar Children series

Hollywood Horror

The movie industry has long linked caving with horror. Among the first films of this type is *Beast from Haunted Cave* (1959). Bank robbers take refuge in a cave, where a spider-like monster attacks them. The tagline for *What Waits Below* (1985) is "Underground, no one can hear you die." American soldiers seeking to rescue a communications team in a Central American cave encounter albino cave dwellers who use the soldiers' body heat to track and kill them. *The Descent* (2005) features six women trapped in an unmapped cave system in North Carolina. They are pursued by flesh-eating, human-like creatures that have lived underground for many centuries. *The Descent II* (2009) begins two days after the close of the original. The survivors return to seek the missing members of their group.

started more than 90 years ago. Written by other authors now, it remains popular with young readers. Number 50, *The Mystery in the Cave* (1995), begins with the four orphans—Benny, Henry, Jessie, and Violet—going into Dragon's Mouth Cavern in search of fossils and precious stones. Benny finds a **sinkhole** that takes them deeper into the cave. They encounter several mysterious people who clearly don't want them there—or to find their way out.

From the beginning, the Floyd Collins saga has exerted a fascination among the general public. Several nonfiction books provide considerable detail about the event. One is *The Life and Death of Floyd Collins*, written by his brother in 1955 and reprinted in 2009. American writer Robert Penn Warren, the only person to receive Pulitzer Prizes in both fiction and poetry, based his 1959 novel *The Cave* on Collins. "*The Cave* is Robert Penn Warren at his best, and they don't come much better than that," noted the *New York Times Book Review*.

The 1951 film *Ace in the Hole* was based in large part on Floyd Collins and even mentions him by name. Reporter Chuck Tatum (played by Kirk Douglas) uses a cave-in that traps Leo Minosa (Richard Benedict) to try to make a name for himself. He convinces the people leading the rescue effort to employ a more dangerous and time-consuming method of drilling because it will keep the story on newspaper front pages and increase

Tatum's fame.

The popular 1920s-era singers Vernon Dalhart and Fiddlin' John Carson released "The Death of Floyd Collins" soon after the tragedy. Grammy-winning folk singer John Prine teamed up with bluegrass artist Mac Wiseman on "Death of Floyd Collins" in 2007. Black Stone Cherry, a Kentucky rock band, recorded "The Ghost of Floyd Collins" the following year.

In 1994, composer/lyricist Adam Guette premiered *Floyd Collins*, a musical about the doomed caver. It won the Louise Lortel Award for best Off-Broadway musical and has been performed in many U.S. theaters and in London, England. Theater critic John Simon said that it is "the original and daring musical of our day ... it is *the* modern musical's true and exhilarating ace in the hole." Every year, a play entitled *The Story of Floyd Collins* is presented in Brownsville, Kentucky, not far from the scene of the tragedy.

Documentary filmmaker Michael Crisp produced *The Death of Floyd Collins* in 2014. The film combines **archival** movie footage, photographs, reenactments, and interviews. Perhaps the most **poignant** interview is with Collins's niece Mildred, who was a toddler at the time of the tragedy. She and her siblings listened to "The Death of Floyd Collins." As she recalled, "One day my daddy [Andy Lee Collins] came home and caught us listening to it, and he took it off the record player and broke it. He didn't like us listening to that song because it brought back bad memories."

Caving also appeals to commercial filmmakers. In 1940, Victor Mature starred in *One Million B.C.* He played Tumak, a cave man who overcomes obstacles to unite the warlike Rock Tribe and the peaceful Shell Tribe. The film was successful at the box office and received Academy Award nominations for its then state-of-the-art special effects and its musical score.

A team of explorers finds a hidden cave in Central Asia in *The Cavern* (2005). They soon encounter supernatural forces that place them in jeopardy. *Journey to the Center of the Earth* (2008) is a sci-fi adventure film that follows the adventures of volcanologist Trevor Anderson (played by Brendan Fraser) and several companions who seek shelter in a cave in Iceland. They fall toward the center of the earth and must escape before time runs out.

The 2011 film *Sanctum*, with actor Rhys Wakefield, follows a group of six underwater cave divers who become trapped in a cavern after a tropical storm blocks their way out.

Sanctum (2011) uses 3D camera techniques pioneered in James Cameron's *Avatar* (2009) to depict the plight of several divers trapped in an underwater cave in Papua New Guinea. Based on a real-life 1988 incident, the film received critical acclaim for its photography.

A man-made cave beneath New York City's historic Trinity Church is a key plot element in *National Treasure* (2004). Benjamin Franklin Gates (Nicolas Cage) discovers a coded message on the back of the Declaration of Independence with directions to a vast horde of treasure hidden during the Revolutionary War. Cage is also a featured voice in the 2013 animated prehistoric cave feature *The Croods*. He plays Grug, the head of a family of cave dwellers. They lose their home during an earthquake and encounter a series of perils as they seek a new home. The film was a box-office hit.

Getting Involved

If you think you might be interested
in caving, probably the best way
to begin is by visiting a show cave.
Many show caves have electric lights
throughout their entire length so you
can easily find your way. Those that
don't, customarily provide lights for
visitors. The path through the cave is
well established. It often goes up and
down stairs, with viewing platforms in
places where the scenery is especially
spectacular. You don't need any

OPPOSITE: Most show caves offer tours led by trained guides.
The guides give information about the cave's history and any
scenic formations along the tour route.

special equipment in most cases, though some caves that haven't been overly developed may require you to either rent a helmet or provide your own. In general, street clothing is acceptable. Athletic shoes or hiking boots are good choices for footwear because they provide better traction on surfaces that may be wet or uneven.

A few show caves are administered by the federal government. These are some of the best known and include Mammoth Cave National Park (Kentucky), Carlsbad Caverns National Park (New Mexico),

Wind Cave National Park (South Dakota), and Oregon Caves National Monument (Oregon). Nearly all others are under private ownership. Both the National Caves Association and U.S. Show Caves Directory maintain lists of show caves.

Many show caves offer group tours. You begin with a brief lecture about the cave system, its history, how it was formed, and what you can expect to see. At some point, your guide is likely to briefly turn out the lights to give you an idea of what the first explorers may have encountered.

Some caves offer special tours for school groups. Many of these include basic caving equipment such as helmets with lights and elbow and knee pads. Even though the gear isn't necessary for the tour, it provides youngsters with hands-on experience with caving gear. These tours

may include sections of the cave that aren't part of the experience for the general public. Students may also have the opportunity to try out cave simulators, in which they twist and turn through a series of interlocking boxes that mimic the narrow passages of real caves.

Some caves offer "off the beaten track" tours that last for several hours. Small groups led by an experienced guide don protective gear and go deeper into the cave's undeveloped sections, often crawling through underground streams, going up and down ladders, **rappelling** down into deep pits, and squeezing through small passageways. Participants can expect to get dirty. As the website for South Dakota's Rushmore Cave notes, "This is a true caving adventure that requires belly crawling through some tight spaces. Our experienced guides will lead you through some areas off of the main tour route that almost no one else sees. This extreme adventure is not for the faint of heart."

No two caverns are alike, and many offer unique features. One of the more intriguing is Indiana's Bluespring Caverns. Tours take place entirely in a small boat cruising slowly along underground streams. The boat itself has the only light, so you can get a sense of the darkness surrounding you. The cavern also offers an overnight adventure that begins with the boat tour. Participants then proceed through an undeveloped portion of the cavern to an underground campsite where they spend the night. Visitors to the Hawaiian island of Maui can experience a different type of cave by exploring the Hana Lava Tube, formed long ago by the volcanoes that helped create the island itself. In New Mexico, you can descend into the Ice Cave, where the temperature never rises above freezing.

Cave Camping

For a truly extreme caving experience, consider cave camping. The chief advantage is being able to conduct extensive explorations deep within a cave system because you're not spending any time getting in and out of the cave every day. Besides the usual caving gear, you'll need a sleeping bag, food, plenty of water, extra clothes, and toilet items. A journal to record your experiences and a book are also desirable. Typically, you'll spend a day getting to your campsite. In the mornings, you eat breakfast, then spend the rest of the day exploring. When you return to camp in the evening, you'll eat dinner, discuss the day's events, and read a little before going to sleep. You clean up the site on the final day and head back out.

The icy floor is more than 20 feet (6.1 m) thick and the deepest portion dates back nearly 3,500 years. In 1897, Colorado's Glenwood Caverns became one of the first American cave systems with electric lighting. A portion of the tours the cave offers are lit with replica lights from that era. Outside the cave, visitors enjoy activities such as thrill rides, laser tag, and a climbing wall.

If visiting one or more show caves—especially if you take one of the adventure tours that so many of them offer—whets your appetite to do more, you need to be aware that unlike participants in many other activities, serious cavers may not welcome you with open arms. Cavers are very protective of their caves. They are afraid that **dilettantes** may be unprepared for the rigors of caving and become lost or injured. They also fear vandals. Few things are more upsetting to cavers than

It's a good idea to make your first caving trips with guides who are familiar with the caves you want to explore.

entering a cave to find that someone has spray-painted their name on the walls. So don't be surprised if you attend a meeting and find that people aren't interested in talking with you. However, if you continue to appear and maintain a respectful attitude, you're likely to find yourself being accepted.

While there are no specific age requirements to go caving, it's not suitable for very young children or elderly adults. Some degree of physical fitness and agility is required, though, as observed elsewhere, cavers learn to go very slowly.

It's a good idea to make your first caving trips with guides who are familiar with the caves you want to ex-

At one time, visitors to California's Corral Canyon Cave could observe American Indian cave paintings and scenic views of Malibu. Now, the cave has been vandalized by graffiti.

plore. They can not only point out things of interest but also warn you about areas that may present difficulties.

As you become more familiar with caving and more comfortable with your abilities, you will likely want to keep pushing your limits. We know that Mt. Everest is the highest point on Earth. We know that the Pacific's Challenger Deep is the deepest point in the oceans. But we don't know for sure if Mammoth Cave and its more than 400 miles (644 km) is the world's longest cave system—or even if it has been completely explored. Cavers are continuously expanding the limits of the cave systems they explore as they seek the thrill of being the first person to discover new passages. Even better, they may unearth entirely new caves. And things don't get much more extreme than that!

Glossary

archival   referring to documents or other types of records of past events

complementary   parts of a larger whole combining to enhance or improve the qualtities of individual components

dilettantes   people with only a superficial interest in an activity or body of knowledge

eulogy   words of praise delivered at a funeral

lyricist   a person who writes words for songs

morbid   excessive interest in disturbing subjects such as death and disease

poignant   causing strong feelings of sadness

rappelling   descending a wall while suspended from a rope

sinkhole   an opening formed in the ground by the action of water that leads to an underground passage

synthetic   describing a material that is not found in nature but created through chemical processes

Selected Bibliography

Aulenbach, Nancy Holler, and Hazel A. Barton. *Exploring Caves: Journeys into the Earth*. Washington, D.C.: National Geographic Society, 2001.

Boga, Steve. *Caving*. Mechanicsburg, Penn.: Stackpole Books, 1997.

Burger, Paul. *Cave Exploring: The Definitive Guide to Caving Technique, Safety, Gear, and Trip Leadership*. Guilford, Conn.: FalconGuides, 2006.

Collins, Homer, and John Lehrberger. *The Life and Death of Floyd Collins*. St. Louis: Cave Books, 2005.

Rea, G. Thomas, ed. *Caving Basics: A Comprehensive Guide for Beginning Cavers*. 3rd ed. Huntsville, Ala.: The National Speleological Society, 1992.

Sparrow, Andy. *The Complete Caving Manual*. Rev. ed. Ramsbury, Wiltshire, UK: Crowood Press, 2011.

Taylor, Michael Ray. *Caves: Exploring Hidden Realms*. Washington, D.C.: National Geographic Society, 2001.

Waltham, Tony. *Great Caves of the World*. Buffalo, N.Y.: Firefly Books, 2008.

Websites

National Caves Association
http://www.cavern.com

The official website of the National Caves Association, a
network of private cave owners, features a directory of private
show caves with complete information, driving directions,
hours of operation, and so forth. Also includes information
about cave origins and development.

National Speleological Society
http://caves.org

The official website of the National Speleological Society
includes news, a calendar of events, lists of local clubs, safety
and techniques, archives of several publications, and more.

Note: Every effort has been made to ensure that any websites listed above were
active at the time of publication. However, because of the nature of the Internet, it is
impossible to guarantee that these sites will remain active indefinitely or that their
contents will not be altered.

Index